PRESENTED TO:

_____

FROM:

_____

DATE:

_____

The Guilt-Free, Mom-Friendly Days of Whine and Noses Journal

Lisa Espinoza Johnson

Copyright © 2004 by John Wiley & Sons, Inc. All rights reserved.

Published by Jossey-Bass
A Wiley Imprint
989 Market Street, San Francisco, CA 94103-1741   www.josseybass.com

No part of this publication may be reproduced, stored in a retrieval system, or transmitted in any form or by any means, electronic, mechanical, photocopying, recording, scanning, or otherwise, except as permitted under Section 107 or 108 of the 1976 United States Copyright Act, without either the prior written permission of the Publisher, or authorization through payment of the appropriate per-copy fee to the Copyright Clearance Center, Inc., 222 Rosewood Drive, Danvers, MA 01923, 978-750-8400, fax 978-646-8600, or on the web at www.copyright.com. Requests to the Publisher for permission should be addressed to the Permissions Department, John Wiley & Sons, Inc., 111 River Street, Hoboken, NJ 07030, 201-748-6011, fax 201-748-6008, e-mail: permcoordinator@wiley.com.

Jossey-Bass books and products are available through most bookstores. To contact Jossey-Bass directly call our Customer Care Department within the U.S. at 800-956-7739, outside the U.S. at 317-572-3986, or fax 317-572-4002.

Jossey-Bass also publishes its books in a variety of electronic formats. Some content that appears in print may not be available in electronic books.

The quotation on page 94 is attributed to Malcolm Muggeridge; the specific source is not known.

ISBN 0-7879-7241-X

Printed in the United States of America
FIRST EDITION
HB Printing 10 9 8 7 6 5 4 3 2 1

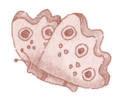

A Message to Moms

About seven years ago, I became inspired to start journaling by a fellow mom who had the most immaculate sets of journals you could imagine—colorful, clever captions penned in perfect handwriting beneath chronologically placed photographs amid pages of poignant descriptions of her life as a mom. She loved the art of handwriting. I can barely *read* my own handwriting and do not particularly enjoy the pen-to-paper process. I was overwhelmed. I knew my limits.

My friend encouraged me to keep it simple and to do only as much as I could realistically maintain and enjoy, in other words to personalize my journaling to fit *me*. So I pulled out a three-ring binder, wrote my kids' names on dividers, and scrawled in black-and-white letters on the front cover "Chase, Chance, and Chandler: Funny Sayings and Stuff." No photos, no colorful captions, very few passages of long, flowery prose, but lots of pages filled with short paragraphs or cryptic phrases meaningful only to members of my family. Like this entry: "8–27–02 CHANDLER—Deodorant on forehead." Everyone in the Johnson home knows that phrase speaks of the time my youngest son, nine-year-old Chandler, put deodorant on his forehead because "that's how they did it on the TV commercial." (They were demonstrating how this particular antiperspirant went on clear, but he didn't get that part.) His older brother Chance, eleven at the time, promptly chimed in to straighten things out, "How dumb. It doesn't go on your forehead. You're supposed to put it on your stomach."

Journaling is truly a personal thing. There is not just *one* way to approach it—no right or wrong way. Maybe you hum a happy tune at the thought of pouring each day's events down to the last giggle into your journal. Or perhaps, like me, your entries are as random as dry pants during potty train-  ing. Maybe you prefer to write directly to your child. For example, one of my entries reads, "7–31–98 CHASE—The other day we said to you, 'Chase, we could never ask for a better first son than you.' You said, 'You could, but then you'd have God on your hands.'" Or maybe you'd rather write for yourself, as if no one else will ever read your words. If you already have your own style of journaling that works for you . . . way to go! Stick with it, girlfriend! If not, here are some suggestions aimed only at priming the pump of your own well of creativity.

1. Keep your journal in a visible place, preferably where your kids are most likely to say or do those things that you absolutely *must* capture for posterity. Easy access is key. And

make sure your writing utensils are nearby. By the way, using specially colored ink is fun, and when something is fun, we're more likely to do it.

2. If you're using multiple journals (one for each child), consider keeping them between bookends in a prominent place or make it a special occasion to go out and choose a container you really like such as a basket or an antique tin. Many moms use multiple journals so that they can pass them on to each child as a keepsake.

3. Should you choose to use one journal for all your children, you might try different ink colors such as pink, green, and purple so as to easily discern who said or did what at a glance. Of course, you could also simply write the child's name next to your journal entry date. I prefer to differentiate *clearly* who said or did what because it proves a handy time-saver when preparing to

blackmail your children as they hit adolescence. I label each entry with the date and the name of the child or children involved.

One thing that always kept me from using those

adorable baby books was the myriad headings and subtitles I was supposed to fill in and could never keep up with (for example, first overnight trip, first pair of shoes, first time to break wind, etc.). This journal is designed to give you the freedom to write what is important to *you*. The quotations and questions are not meant to be strict guidelines for what to write on each page. Their purpose is to encourage you as a mom and to inspire you in your journaling. Whether related to the writing prompts or your own random recollections of the day, whether penned as poetic paragraphs or snappy snippets, your entries, in your own style, should grace these pages.

If you just aren't able to keep up with your journal for a while, and you're feeling like, "What's the use? I've dropped the ball," remember the goal is not perfection (said the perfectionist to her fellow moms). The goal is to capture some wonderful memories. Just start again when you can and go from there.

Mothering can lead us down a path of tremendous personal and spiritual growth. That's why this journal has two parts. In the first, entitled Here's to Me, you will encounter questions

as well as inspirational sayings from my book *Days of Whine and Noses: Pep Talks for Tuckered-Out Moms*. These are aimed at encouraging you to explore your own thoughts and feelings about mothering and life in general. The second part, Here's to You, focuses on the hilarious and heartwarming antics of your children. In years to come, you will pull out your journal and reread your words and marvel at how motherhood shaped and molded you in ways you could never have dreamed. You will recognize the profound lessons learned in the often mundane routines of mothering. You will see how just as your children were growing up, so were you.

As moms, we tend to feel guilty about *everything*. This journal is *not* intended to serve as one more opportunity for you to exercise your guilt muscle. I'll be the first to admit that there are times when my journal entries are separated by more than a few major holidays. That's OK.

A Message to Moms

The purpose of this journal is to nurture you as a mom, so decide now to enjoy the journey and give the guilt muscle a rest. Heed my wise friend's advice—keep it simple and only do what you are able to maintain and enjoy. Here's to a journey like none other—these wild and wonderful Days of Whine and Noses!

Here's to Me

It's so easy to get lost in the all-encompassing role of motherhood. But consider this. Before you were a mom, you were a woman. What does that woman love to do?

Apple Juice and Ah-Ha Moments

> The God who gave me these energetic kids understands my struggles and limitations. He will meet me on my turf—my sticky, apple-juice-stained turf.

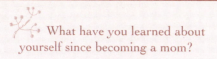

What have you learned about yourself since becoming a mom?

Way to Grow

> Each of us has our own personal décor, the décor of our life. It's called character, and it's what people remember about us.

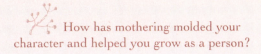

How has mothering molded your character and helped you grow as a person?

When I Need Soul Food I . . .

> When you rock your
> little one, breathing in
> the sweet aroma of Cheerios
> and paradise, breathing
> out the prayer of gratitude,
> you nourish your soul.

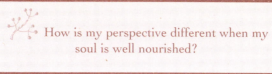

How is my perspective different when my soul is well nourished?

Is It Bedtime Yet?

> A word of encouragement is refreshment for a weary soul, a moment of beauty in the midst of a trying day.

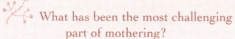

What has been the most challenging part of mothering?

That's What Friends Are For

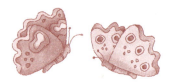

> It's so important to
> spend time with others
> like ourselves who get it,
> who know firsthand this
> round-the-clock roller coaster
> of life with little people.

> In what ways do your connections with others enhance you personally and in your mothering?

Bibs, Binkies, and Daily Blessings

> God says "I love you" in so many ways... the soft breath of a newborn baby, the warmth of a glowing sunrise, the timely word of encouragement from a friend.

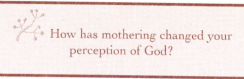

How has mothering changed your perception of God?

The Other-Than-a-Mother Dream

> Psychologists Henry Cloud and John Townsend in their book *Boundaries with Kids* say, "Kids with parents who have a life learn both that they aren't the center of the universe and that they can be free to pursue their own dreams."

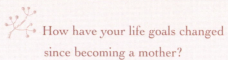

How have your life goals changed since becoming a mother?

As Good as It Gets

> By living with one foot poised anxiously on tomorrow, we rob ourselves of the ability to truly live today.

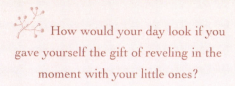

> How would your day look if you gave yourself the gift of reveling in the moment with your little ones?

Here's to You

Children view the world through clear lenses. Free of inhibitions, they simply and innocently experience the wonders of their world.

You Make Me Laugh!

> Kids don't give a rip what anyone thinks. They pull on that Superman mask and cape and away they go bounding and leaping down the toilet paper aisle, just lovin' life.

Treasure of My Heart

> We love these little people so much, not because of their accomplishments or their exemplary behavior (as any mother of a two-year-old can attest). They are precious to us simply because they are our children.

My Tiny Teacher

> These days of whine and noses offer us the richest lessons of life—a deeper meaning than meets the eye.

You're a Genius!

> Nothing lies outside a child's knack for transforming the common into the novel.

When You Grow Up I Hope You . . .

> We are fulfilling a
> God-given purpose
> when we use our skills, our
> hands, and our
> imaginations to leave
> our own unique,
> indelible mark on the day.

I'm Still
Ten Shades of Red
from When You . . .

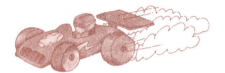

> It does my heart good in a demented sort of way to hear stories of other parents who've been similarly embarrassed by their children.

You've Changed My Life!

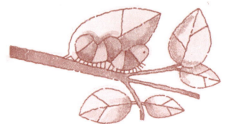

> Change can be a
> rewarding experience
> if we are willing to
> step forward with open arms
> to welcome the new
> possibilities before us.

You Love to Play . . .

Kids *can* and *will* make their own toys out of anything they find lying around the house. Every family photo album contains pictures of Junior sitting contentedly in an empty box while his brand new scooter sits unoccupied somewhere in the background.

My Prayer for You . . .

_____

_____

_____

_____

_____

_____

_____

_____

_____

_____

> When a grain of sand irritates the oyster, a process is set into motion. Eventually the end result of this gradual process is a beautiful pearl hiding within the oyster's shell. Trust the process.

Treasure of My Heart

> I welcome the familiarity and intimacy that ushers my eleven-year-old to the threshold of my bathroom to ask through the door, "Mom, do you want to play Scrabble?"

My Tiny Teacher

> Malcolm Muggeridge said, "Every happening in life great or small is a parable whereby God is speaking to you. And the art of life is to get the message."

It's Been a Looonnnggg Day!

> Next time you're greeted by a doozy of a mess, don't be surprised. Look at it simply as a reminder that you are alive and well on planet Earth."

From the Mouths of Babes...

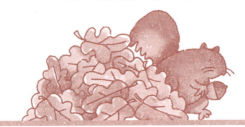

> "Mom, guess what? If you turn out the light and rub your hands really hard on your pants legs, you can see sparks!"

You're a Genius!

> The eyes of a child
> can look upon the
> most common of everyday
> objects and infuse them
> with limitless potential.

When You Grow Up I Hope You . . .

> There are those among us who have grown up but have managed to retain the freedom of childhood to be who they are regardless of the tide of public opinion.

I'm Still
Ten Shades of Red
from When You . . .

> People who don't
> take themselves or
> their children's inevitable
> "pick the nose and eat it"
> incidents too seriously have
> an ease about them that
> allows others to loosen
> up and laugh as well.

How'd You Do That!???

> When it comes to creativity, our best teachers live right in our own homes.

You've Changed My Life!

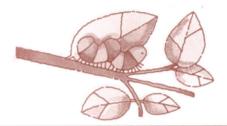

Anything worthwhile
  comes at a cost.

You Love to Play . . .

> Given no
> preconceived notions
> of what goes where, these
> little ones throw open the doors
> of possibility and exploration!

My Prayer for You . . .

> You are of infinite value simply because you are marked with the fingerprints of your Creator.

About the Author

Lisa Espinoza Johnson is a humorist, recording artist, writer, and speaker known for her down-to-earth humor and practical insights. Her album, "Candy Kisses, Muddy Hugs," and her first book, *Days of Whine and Noses: Pep Talks for Tuckered-Out Moms* are by turns hilarious and heart-warming, and both are sources for encouragement for moms.

Lisa and her husband, Chip, live in Southern California with their four energetic kids: three sons and a surprise baby *girl!* You can find out more about Lisa at
www.candykissesmuddyhugs.com.